Second Edition

THE WIND HAS A VOICE

tate publishing
CHILDREN'S DIVISION

SANDRA LOTT

Published by Tate Publishing & Enterprises, LLC
127 E. Trade Center Terrace | Mustang, Oklahoma 73064 USA
1.888.361.9473 | www.tatepublishing.com

Tate Publishing is committed to excellence in the publishing industry. The company reflects the philosophy established by the founders, based on Psalm 68:11,
"The Lord gave the word and great was the company of those who published it."

Book design copyright © 2015 by Tate Publishing, LLC. All rights reserved.
Cover and interior design by Eileen Cueno
Illustrations by Kenneth rede Rikimaru

Published in the United States of America
ISBN: 978-1-63418-345-1
1. Religion / Christian Ministry / General
2. Religion / Christian Ministry / Children
14.12.08

This book belongs to:

· ·

Do you ever wonder if God Speaks to you?

Do you ever wonder how?

Read on and you might find out!

The wind was blowing gently, just enough to stir the leaves on the ground. It was a sunny day with a few fluffy white clouds scattered through the sky.

Gerald Ray and Timmy were walking through the park. They had just finished playing ball with their friends and were on their way home. But they were not quite ready to go home. The two brothers decided to sit by the small pond and skip stones across the water.

"Wow! That was a good one!" Gerald Ray shouted. *Timmy was always good at skipping stones, he thought to himself.*

Timmy and Gerald Ray oddly enough got along pretty good most of the time. They were two years apart, Timmy being nine, he was the oldest and had hair the color of autumn's burnt orange leaves. Gerald Ray was seven and had hair the color of sun-kissed gold.

Already bored, the boys sat by the water and looked at the fish splashing here and there.

"Look at that one!" Timmy yelled, grinning from ear to ear. "I wish I had my fishing pole!" Tim added as he watched another one splash.

Just about that time, Gerald Ray caught sight of the leaves blowing to and fro, and it seemed to make him wonder how the wind could rustle the leaves so, and yet you couldn't see it like you could the rain.

He was a little too quiet, and Timmy, always having something to say, asked, "What ya so quiet for?"

"I was just looking at those leaves; see how the wind blows them all around?" Gerald Ray asked.

"Yeah, so what?" Timmy said.

With a puzzled look on his face, Gerald Ray asked, "How come the wind can blow those leaves and make such a mess like it did with the storm last week, but you can't see it?"

"I don't know. It just is, sort of like God, you know, like we learned in Sunday school" Timmy answered.

"What do you mean?" Gerald Ray asked.

"Well," Timmy started as they sat in the grass watching the tree branches above blowing over them, "there has to be a God. The world just didn't appear one day. Like the cake Mom made last week. I don't like cooking, but I was bored so I watched her make it. She put all this stuff in a bowl and mixed it up, and then she dumped it into a pan and baked it. When it was done, boy did it smell good! She slapped my hand as I tried to sneak a piece and said I had to wait."

Gerald Ray got impatient. "What does that have to do with God?" he asked.

"Well, if you would let me finish, I'll tell you," Timmy yelled. He went on. "She mixed things up and made that cake. It didn't just appear. It made me think of our Sunday school lesson, and I sort of understood. There had to be someone to make the world too, just like the cake.

"You can't see God, but he's there. The world is proof. It was made just like the cake. You can't see the wind, but it is there. You see what it does," Timmy finished.

"Wow!" Gerald Ray exclaimed with a look of pride in his eyes. He always looked up to his big brother. "I never thought of that."

They started back home shoving and pushing each other along the way. You could almost see the thoughts of their conversation swirl around in the back of Gerald Ray's mind.

Sunday was here, and everyone was getting ready for church. Timmy was pounding on the bathroom door. Even at the age of seven, Gerald Ray had to have his hair look just right.

"Hurry up! Why do you got to lock the door? What ya doing in there?" Timmy yelled as he danced from foot to foot.

"I'm combing my hair and brushing my teeth!" Gerald Ray yelled back.

"You don't have to lock the door to do that! Come on! Open up!" Timmy shouted.

"Boys, we are going to be late. Stop that arguing and get dressed! Now!" Dad's voice rumbled through the hallway.

They were on their way, and Gerald Ray was looking out the window. It was still windy outside, and a lot more clouds were in the sky.

Once inside, everyone was getting settled. Gerald Ray sat in his chair by the window with Timmy right behind him. He kept looking outside. Somehow what Timmy had said the day before really stuck in his head.

"Class," the teacher called out, "sit down and open up your Sunday school lesson. She continued, "Today we are reading about Noah's ark."

Gerald Ray sat there and listened while the teacher went on. He was so curious now that things were starting to make a little bit more sense. The teacher went on as she read about how the storm roared outside the ark. She said that though the storm roared, Noah and his family were all safe inside. The whole class loved Miss Ellie. They all sat and listened intently as she read on. She had a way of making a story come to life.

Later that day, Timmy asked Gerald Ray if he wanted to go fishing at the pond. That was one of Timmy's favorite pastimes besides baseball. Off they went. Mom yelled out the door, "Don't be too late! We are eating an early dinner today."

The wind was still rustling the leaves and with a little bit more power. It even whistled a few times.

It made Gerald Ray think even more as he thought of their dad that morning shouting through the hallway for them to stop arguing. *You couldn't see Dad, yet you could hear his voice. You couldn't see the wind, yet you could hear it whistle.*

Settling in at their favorite spot, they started to bait their lines. "Tim, I can't get mine. Will you do it?" Gerald Ray asked.

"Just a minute, let me finish mine," Timmy said.

They sat there with their lines in the water, and the fish weren't biting. Gerald Ray's mind was racing again. "Why are you so quiet?" Timmy asked.

"I was thinking about what you said yesterday about God, not seeing him, yet he's real anyway. We heard Dad yell this morning and we couldn't see him. We heard the wind whistle as it blew the leaves.

"Well, can we hear God even though we can't see him?" Gerald Ray said.

"You thought about all that?" Timmy said. Timmy sat there and thought.

It never occurred to him before to think that God had a voice, but why not? You could hear the wind. He thought and he thought, and then it came to him! Miss Ellie told them that God is love. He is all things beautiful, he is Peace, he is our Provider, Protector, and Savior. He remembered how safe he felt in his mother's arms when he was scared during the storm last week. It thundered, and lightning filled the sky. They were afraid when the lights went out. Mom came and held them while Dad checked the fuse box.

"I got it!" Timmy shouted. "Remember," he went on, "how Miss Ellie told us that God is love and how he is our provider, protector, and savior?"

"Yeah," Gerald Ray said as he sat there listening intently.

"Well," Timmy went on, "Mom made us feel safe in that storm last week. She loves us and I don't understand how, but she even says it is out of love when she spanks us when we don't listen to her. I don't understand that. Love isn't supposed to hurt that much! I think God's voice is in the love people show. His voice is in their heart, and since he made the world and he is our Provider and Protector, it seems to me that he has to tell the wind, the rain, and the snow what to do to keep things growing so we can have food. He has to tell them what to do to keep us safe, sort of like God's voice is also in the wind. Since he is God, his voice can be everywhere."

Gerald Ray sat back and smiled. "Yeah!" he said, now it all seemed to fit. "Tim! Look out! You have a bite on your line!" he shouted.

It was getting late. They started back home, fish and fishing poles in hand. They both looked on as they walked through the park watching the leaves blowing in the wind.

THE END

The truth of God's Word tells of how God speaks to us

God speaks to our hearts through the Holy Spirit, as said in the book of John in the Bible. "But when He, the Spirit of Truth, comes, He will guide you into all truth. He will not speak on His own; He will speak only what He hears, and He will tell you what is yet to come. He will bring glory to Me by taking from what is Mine and making it known to you. All that belongs to the Father is Mine. That is why I said the Spirit will take from what is Mine and make it known to you" (John 16:13–15).

You will know by the warmth in your heart just as the disciples felt as they talked with the already-risen Lord. "Were not our hearts burning within us while He talked with us on the road and opened the Scriptures to us?" (Luke 24:32).

God also speaks through His written Word. "In the beginning was the Word, and the Word was with God, and the Word was God. He was with God in the beginning" (John 1:1–2). The Word of God is Jesus Christ. "The Word became flesh and made His dwelling among us. We have seen His glory, the glory of the One and Only, who came from the Father, full of grace and truth" (John 1:14).

God also speaks to us in our dreams. "He said, 'Listen to My words: When a prophet of the Lord is among you, I reveal Myself to him in visions, I speak to him in dreams. But this is not true of My servant Moses; he is faithful in all My house. With him I speak face to face, clearly and not in riddles; he sees the form of the Lord'" (Numbers 12:6–9).

Whether it is a knowing in your heart or a verse in the Bible that jumps off the page, and warmth fills your heart or a dream, when God speaks to you in any of these ways, you will know it.

 **LIVE**

listen|imagine|view|experience

AUDIO BOOK DOWNLOAD INCLUDED WITH THIS BOOK!

In your hands you hold a complete digital entertainment package. In addition to the paper version, you receive a free download of the audio version of this book. Simply use the code listed below when visiting our website. Once downloaded to your computer, you can listen to the book through your computer's speakers, burn it to an audio CD or save the file to your portable music device (such as Apple's popular iPod) and listen on the go!

How to get your free audio book digital download:

1. Visit www.tatepublishing.com and click on the e|LIVE logo on the home page.
2. Enter the following coupon code:
   710b-a53b-0d35-3329-706e-e1be-df4b-9b39
3. Download the audio book from your e|LIVE digital locker and begin enjoying your new digital entertainment package today!